MUSKERRY

by

ROBERT WELCH

The Dedalus Press
24 The Heath, Cypress Downs, Dublin 6W

ISBN 0 948268 93 X (paper)
ISBN 0 948268 94 8 (bound)

Cover design by Niamh Foran based on
"The Valley Thick with Corn" by Samuel Palmer (1805-1881).

Grateful acknowledgement is made to the editors of the following:
*Cyphers, Irish University Review, The Honest Ulsterman,
PN Review, Poetry and Audience, Poetry Ireland Review,
New Irish Writing, The Salmon, Writing Ulster.* My profound
thanks to Archie Markham.

The Dedalus Press receives financial assistance from
An Chomhairle Ealaíon, The Arts Council, Ireland.

Clóchur: Peanntrónaic Teo.
Printed by: Colour Books Ltd.

CONTENTS

for Angela

TO SAINT GOBNAIT

Mover in the fair of sensations,
lady of the beekeepers,
watcher of the engines and the turbines,
stillness of February warmth
early morning in your valleys;
protect the ventures of your people
in Muskerry and Iveleary,
wherever they go
on the dark and bright slopes
of the world.

THE FEAR ORCHARD

She did not like them, much,
when they were there,
but liked them less
as they were going away.

She reasoned at noon
when the gong was struck for lunch:
"I do not like their pity
nor my own expectation.

"I shall write biographies of the unborn,
and watch their lives
collide with fact
and show how gradually they tire."

Once there had been a voice
saying she could not be distracted,
but it was long ago,
and had she heard correctly?

Fear was now relentless
and fierce: a steel triangle
hanging in an orchard
glinting in blue smoke.

THE LOUGH ROAD

1.

The Woman

She got up at eight, swam to breakfast
through the thickening fog.

By half past nine the table had begun to move,
the bread to eat her innards.

She wanted to devour the curtains
out of fury.

At noon the room was turning,
accelerating into what became for her
its cruising speed.

By afternoon her hair was white,
and the priest from the Lough Chapel
eyed her with alarming eyes,
thinking to himself,
inside his sad black serge:
"This is the mother and father of a difficulty."

2.

The Priest

Next day, dressing for Mass,
he thought how much he liked
the cold touch of the vestments on his skin
which was always hot.

A white suddenness raced through him
like electricity.

He made his motions more deliberate,
and the tingling went out.

Later, when he broke the bread,
he didn't like its jagged edge too much.

LADY WILDE

After her husband went mad
at last she wrote the meditations,
calling them her *Passions,* in a room
filled with calm Victorian light.

Next door, in his surgery,
her husband once more was filing
the edges of his scalpels.

Her sentence cut through time
as it rested between two loud thuds
of the grandfather clock.

Her grief and that of her son
would be, she knew, so great,
as to wake the dog that watches
to devour the souls of the dead.

BIRMINGHAM 1916

The breath was white
in the air before her
when she woke.
The windowpanes were frosted up again.

On each side of her her sisters
and in the lower half of the bed
three brothers. The smallest
held in his fist above the blanket,
and close to his face, a ball
made of paper scraps,
criss-crossed with thread and string.

Downstairs her mother shouted,
driving at her father.
Later she'd stand outside the factory gate
and wait for bits of bread,
an applecore, from the workers
as they came out from night shift.

She moved up closer to her sister's back.
Everywhere her like were multiplying her like:
a thought to hold to, in the indifference,
as through frosty glass a ray of sun.

HERMETICA
'Nothing's more capacious than the incorporeal.'

Go back again and this time speak out,
with no explanation or apology.
Stand before the two of them
and don't be unmanned by their vanishing.

You know they're out there. Just because you can't
point them out to the incurious
is no reason for distrusting what you've known
all along the sunless days.

So now, go back and say to them:
the time is come for both of you, father and son,
to go off into whatever next you can invent.
What it will be will be as you have made it.

Don't hang around here. This yard
is now my threshing ground,
to make of it what I can; your time is past.
Your memory continues only to make us sorrow.

And what use is our pity for you?
It won't reach you out there, save on a wave
of emotion, touching you slightly,
like night air on the face of a soldier

staggering from a brothel, the brief respite
before return to duty, insult,
and the harsh details. Go on now,
you're ready; you've been so for a long time.

Meantime this yard's my threshing ground.
If I neglect it I'll end up confused,
confusing others, just like you two, thinking
you should be there still every Friday

counting out the pound notes and shillings,
licking the gummed brown envelopes,
thinking of supper in the growing dark,
with conversation and the aroma of women.

THE MARIE CELINE

Sucking at her nipple
he soothes her blood.
His pull comforts
her bones and the
slack skin in folds
across her stomach.

Somewhere a door
slams in the white
corridor. Quiet deepens.
His eyes open: slits
of pure blue as he drives
his mouth into her soft flesh.

On all fours in the nursing
ward a cleaner scrubs
terracotta tiles. The brush
sloshes easily through
thickening foam. Her grimed
hand is beautiful.

SPEECHIFYING AND THE BREAKING OF IT

You, you threatened
always (giving the notion
that there was a reserve)
that you would be
the way you were
never, ever to be.

You spoke off a gloomy
platform into a sea
of faces tilted upwards
to you. You were good.
They were quiet. You
kept them tranced.

Stiffnecked, they loved
your polysyllables, your
famous furious bark,
the outrageousness of its
intolerance, and, weekly,
they came back for more.

Helicopters you ranted about,
and the napalm of the love
which is war. That they'd
only be themselves by
flailing at the enemy
in the extreme purity of rage.

All this was said before
the night you wandered
by the river's edge, and saw
for the first time, really saw
the eider ducks in flight
heading for the Arctic.

And it was before the afternoon
at the year's end when
you looked through a gap
in the sandhills and saw the Bann,
grey as the centuries, opening
out into turbulent sea.

JUDAS
"one of you is a devil" John VI 70

It is a small field at the back;
stony, tired soil; a tree.
Stole out at four to look
at the bank of cloud.

Cool, but he was sweating
as he gazed up at the branches;
on the ground, beside the trunk
a pitcher, with a grimy handle.

This is the place he'll come to
again and again, to think out
ways of ceasing. No use anymore
to talk to friend or lover.

What had been done, by him,
was too strong to take; not just
the betrayal, the shock that it was him,
and that the Master had prepared.

He'd not forget that look, or the gentle
arm through his. But worse worse
the hurt in the eyes of her who'd
cried tears when she washed the feet.

Her sorrow was all shy timid things: voles,
hares, mice, badgers; the tomcat trapped
in the garage for days, the overhead metal door
having slammed. All he was was a roar.

TO A FRIEND WHO HAS BEEN ATTACKED

I can see him, bleating
in the archive.
Harsh fingernails lengthening
to talons for the forage;
turning over, with a relish,
each leaf, each page,
salivating. Salivating.

His breath gets shorter as he hunts,
his quarry all his own invention.
His ferocity reveals the text
he wishes he could write:
a text with no conjunctions,
all interaction gone,
no hankering, no instinct for
surprise, interrogation,
need.

Stone may help you to forgive.

Such a text confounds
all conversation, is
the grid-pattern of a city
constructed for the dead;
each dwelling a steel
structure with a grille
to keep the umlauts in,
the pronouns and substantive verbs.

Where are all the moods, conditions,
the interactions of phenomena?
Look again: see how
across the plain in front of Tara
light comes once more
to show the harsh striation
on the stone: each loop
and spiral turns another one
around into itself.

Thought is there to test the weight
of time as felt and seen.
It moves and shifts
to catch the shadings of what is.
Only fantasists insist.
Realists offer to us, if we hold,
referential guides, that move,
to actual stone, that is.

Stone may help you to forgive.

MEDITATIONS ON THE SUBJECT OF HONOUR

I

At the graveside he nodded slightly
and his men gathered round
to protect the husband assailed
by a crowd of sympathizers.
There was bright sunlight and hardly
any noise. He was standing back
blinking in the sunlight his olive eyes.
Later I saw him walking down the road
eating an ice cream, talking.

II

I went to see him at his house:
a three-bedroomed council semi
on a new estate. Relaxed and easy
he spoke freely at the formica table
as we drank dark tea.
He didn't ask me what I came for
but we talked about insult
and how it's dealt with.
How, sometimes, you can chasten.
Sometimes not.

III

After that I'd call in now and again.
If he'd not be there his sister
would make me welcome.
It had never been possible before
to think I had a family,
but here, in this house, privacy
and quiet made conversation avid
and free. Once, for a long time,
she looked at me without speaking
and then said, very slowly:
"how do you like this place?"
"Fine, I like it fine."

IV

I was unused to intimate subtlety
having come from the educated world
of bad statements, emotion and talk.
Here, at the blue formica table
there weren't intrusions. In the other world
of threats, resignations, weeping,
men would talk of 'doing' someone,
or of 'getting' him. But such speech,
I now began to see, was just
a caterwaul of the pathetic and destroyed.
Here there was no excess, merely
the slow recognition of what,
it would be gradually agreed,
was becoming inevitable.

V

In that other world of libraries,
commentary, interpretation
they got around, with terrific haste,
to morality, justice, impartiality,
even as they thought of blood.
Here, in this pacific house,
there was never the desire to blame.

COUVADE
(for Liz McIntyre)

Who is out there on the harsh postings
on the lookout for us? As, in the meantime,
we lie abed nursing grievances,
memories of wrongs done
to us or which we've done.
At this stage of vacancy,
so strong the urgings of pain,
we are not sure about blame.
We discuss endlessly and argue:
each man lying on a pallet
inside the large earthwork.
Conversations proceed that rehearse
the dialogues we will have
when death comes. Now fear
mostly keeps the disputes going
as pain enlivens livid flesh.

Is there someone there on the lookouts?
Our protectors were down to one,
but that was long ago,
and we could not be sure
about the energetic messenger,
he who came in, shouting
and congratulating himself
for his tempestuousness, his
(what did someone say?) 'address'.

What hurt brought us here,
what division? Our instructors
had said, always, that secrets
should be hoarded. This appealed
because we were secretive anyway:
that gave us ascendancy over the toiling others,
who blathered incoherencies.
But the day came: harsh light
shining down, metal dully gleaming,
the horses ready for the race,
and she between them, shouting, promising
disgrace, disgrace, disgrace.

Something in us then wanted all the mischief out,
made love to her curses, loved our shame.

THE GOOD MARRIAGE
(for the Courtneys)

The mirror's plaque of quiet
transmitting, still,
in the dining room,
the faces he assumed
for the long walk
to Pouladuff,
and the silence he would wear
for her, no longer
in the easy chair.

THE 'PAV': 1967

Saturday evenings in the Pavilion
Restaurant. Dinner at 8.00 p.m.
We'd still be quiet from the peace
of being together since 6.00 o'clock.
Evening now really settling in. The long
Cork evenings, with the air stilled,
even though this was the main street
we were looking down upon. Huge red
curtains swept up from the crimson
carpet; across the dining room,
a coal fire burned, though not because
of cold. This would be October,
maybe, with our lives before us,
a winter of maturity ahead
bestowing now, upon our silence,
a gravity of joy and tenderness.
There is fear and there is failure,
and there is hope, too;
not much else to say of those quiet
evenings, full of darkening light,
that would not be intrusion.

DEATHWEAVE

Though men were buried there as well
it was a cemetery for women;
lacemakers, who, when living, had a spell

to keep their fingers certain
after death, so they could work
memory into pictures of their men.

A picture holds to work
upon him there, stripped down
to a skeleton in the dark

house of remorseful bone.
This place a shudder he's
known before: marrow to his pain.

Now begins the pattern of release:
dragged from longing, once again
he's forced up onto his knees

through her transmission
working down. Active, light,
it infiltrates the flagstone.

She's weaving a bobbin-net
of recollection, her memory blazing,
which pulls him to her. He cries out,

involved so much with light it makes him sing
the air's live distances, their lessening.

SO FAR, SO HIGH

A high wide roof, and above,
the sky: it is somewhere in Europe
before the wars, the two big ones,
this century. A station, perhaps,
or a place of waiting. Air's
clear and light in the lungs,
a smart awareness all through
the blood. He and she stand,
under the glass canopy
way above their heads. They
are going higher up, to where
the air is purer still and thin,
so thin you'd hear a sigh
from the far side of the valley.
He turns to her (or is it she
to him?) and hearts beat
more slowly now than ever before.
Soon they will be, almost, still.

A HOUSE OF THE KEARNEYS

in memory of Kathleen Kearney
died June 1989

"...a house of the Kearneys, where the father
and mother died, but it was well known
that they came back to look after the children."

(W.B.Yeats, noted down in
Co. Galway by Lady Gregory
and himself, 1897)

I

Your power is totally direct emotion,
which you can use to burn through
door after door of guile,
but you were rarely satisfied,
suspecting there might not *be*
a core to get at.

Suspecting which, did you trust?
You loved the dead, protected
in their stillness and loved them
more and more, valuing their
lack of guile, their power,
which you had seen in action.

Your brother Tom, riddled with cancer in
St Finbarr's, got up and walked
straight out, hoping that your mother
would look after him, just as
she lifted out from his spine
the hard black ball when he was a child.

II

"There is no desire that cannot be fulfilled
if only the price is paid." That was what
the man said in Musgrave's well before
your own time.

But the secret is that the price may well
be paid by the one who suffers, not the crowing male
that satisfies himself, then goes about
the business.

In suffering everything becomes secret; even
the smallest venture, buying a frock
or pair of shoes, is fraught with danger.
The heart's all hunger.

Suspicion is everywhere. You saw
your father low over the cranking handle
of a Crossley Tender; his thin body so frail
how could he not go blind?

Everything burned with malevolence in the corner shop:
the smell of bread, the rich savour of smoked ham,
the array of cakes in the wooden tray, all
charged with hate.

Now you're going over again that sure moment
of actual blessing. It was September, the leaves were going,
and you pushing open the green gate in Bishopstown;
he standing in the doorway.

You are five or six once more; he's in black,
your grandfather with the big Fermoy moustache;
his teeth whiten through the smoky hair;
there are apples in the orchard.

III

They'd never speak the word,
but mouth it in the air,
with eyes averted in alarm
in case the kids would listen in,
or the disease itself.

My mother and my grandmother
sitting in the dark kitchen,
having tea. I on one
of the tubular stools
with its Dunlopillo cushion
straining, as ever, to hear.

They'd not say the name
and I would be drawn into
this terror lanced with fear:
"when they opened him he was red
rotten so they just stitched him up again."

"When the air gets at it
that's the end of the story.
Goodbye then."

IV

At what point or place or hour
did the dark slip into her delicate brain
to cloud her eyes?

Perhaps some day going up Summerhill South
she stopped to look at the Reparation Convent
and thought of her own exposed and open life.

Her childhood had seen too little praise.
A kind nun had praised her English and her sewing,
but mostly there was ferocity.

The dark slipped in perhaps on such an afternoon
where a mind dared to think its life:
a harsh rope slung across a ravine

in a black night. The black night
boiling with sudden shocks of chill,
spasms of fire across an unprotected face.

She reads aloud late at night

Just a few days before Christmas,
very late on a Thursday night,
my father not yet in
from his day shift in Dunlop's,
there was a sense of empty space.

I left my bed to go to her, carrying with me
a book of fairy stories, with small pictures,
just black lines, red spots, black splotches;
and of these the illustrator made
a world of elves, toadstools with doors
and chimneys, small bearded fellows
looking out of windows at us, grinning,
tiny pipes in their mouths, sleeves rolled up.

We lay there, in the warm bed,
the sidelamp on, and she read to me
the stories; and I watched them happen
in this little white and red and black world,
completely peopled now. I was able to hear
the small hum a little set of lives would make.

And nothing happened at all. These were
different stories to the ones so often favoured,
full of bright actions and terrible journeys.
These were quiet, but charged with absolute delight.
Curtains there were sheets of white with big red dots.

Sometime later we heard the gate swing in the dark
and my father's key in the front door lock
He came into the bedroom smiling and she said:
"You're drunk"; which he did not deny.
There was little more than a mild reproach
to chill the warm and comfortable joy.

VI

In bed she heard a faint knock.
No one else had heard it,
and she knew that no one would.
She came down, in the cool
of the dark, to let her grandmother in.

For a long time it had been raining,
and the old woman was drenched,
two rivulets ran from a tangle
of hair above her ears as she came in
through the back door into the light.

From Bishopstown she brought with her
three gifts, to be given at the dead of night:
honey and salt and milk, — with a small
sea shell, from which they should be taken.

The honey was to keep the flesh wholesome,
the salt to clear the eye, and the milk
would serve to calm the mind in face of death.
She was told she would forget this night visit,
until the very end when she would need all three.

VII

After you have gone
everything is still once more.
You looked up the white stairs
to the landing where I stood,
and your heart failed.

Forget the white paint,
the perfect finish of the Artex,
the polished brasses holding
the bloodred carpet. Outlined
in light from the window behind,
you saw me there.

In the sallow evening, across
the Evergreen Road, the nuns
walked along the high parapet
of the convent, saying the rosary.
The world was full of such details.
You, bravely, tried to manage a few,
a small few, but as the years went
there was less and less.

A white painted stairs, brass
fastners, and a calm light;
one evening while the nuns
prayed and walked in gold.

INISCARRA

"When ... anarchy presents itself as a
danger to us, we know not where to turn."
Matthew Arnold

The riverbank at Iniscarra of a
summer evening. The languid turn
of the water. Inhale the dark
mystery as you stand on the shale
of the riverbank. Take in, too,
the little crypt adjoining the tiny
Church of Ireland. The long embrasures
are unglassed, its dark open to the air.
A cool republic of the twilight in there
where everything resolves, felt on the hand,
which you can slip through the stone lips.

Out here there's a brief respite
in the air above the river before
it heads down to the city and division.
Slowly light thickens and the vapour
glistens with points of malice. Formulating
itself, a head translates itself from mist,
darkening further air already darkened.

> *forget polite thin souls*
> *no overcoats for Burberry days*
> *they're threadbare anyways*
> *with effort of candour stuff*
> *devotion snapoff*
> *who's managing who or whom?*
> *think it out or not but*
> *comply comply comply*

The tiny face consigns itself again
to the gathering dark; its speech
fades into the gurgling of the water
over the black stones. Downstream,
a little further, a sandbank
interrupts the steady flow to the city.
Just barely, on the spit that separates
the flood I see the old friend of my youth,
arms raised, calling out, his voice
at first no more than a trouble
in the water's heavier vexation,
but rising to a steady tone,
an authority over the water
driving into stone and rock and gravel.

> remember the cold friend
> the one at the crossroads where
> privet flowers sheds its
> totally normal perfumes
> still there still here
> watch for possibles signs?
> fear absolute uncertainty
> a total slowdown and loss of
> nerve then then he
> (that's me)'s there here

ROSEBAY WILLOWHERB

Fireweed burns along the bank
of the river Wharfe; paths
are thick heavy sludge, black
and intense; the boot sinks
into the yielding, each trudge
sucks itself. Solemnity
is the stubble running from
river path to the barred gate
away across the open field.
England is so sad. Otley
sighs; you can see its unfired
smokestacks cresting the iron
viaduct upstream. The long stalks
of rosebay willowherb ignite
the strenuous dark grey
colorations. Forlorn and exquisite
these Sundays at the end
of the long and powerful decline.

LOWER CONGRESS ROAD, 1958

Living so closely with each other
they seemed involved in silence;
between the old lady and the boy
there was much absence, and he'd look
for a long time, when he came in from school,
at the check oilcloth, parcelling
the kitchen's light and dark.
Out the back there were the two mass-concrete
stanchions of the clothesline,
the wild back gardens and their wintry grasses.

MEMOIRS OF A KERRY PARSON

I

In the evenings I would fumble in my loneliness,
colliding with the furniture
in the darkened parlour.

Sometimes I would try
to character the past,
but never got beyond the opening lines:

*The Bishop of Limerick thought the spires of Protestant
churches would civilize the County of Kerry. That
severe elegance, he thought, would serve to...*

Always the continuing end.
My tongue would arch for speech,
but readiness would dissolve
in contemplation of a lichen stain
on the greyness of my boundary wall.

II

Her face that evening at my leaded panes.
Did her skin derive its texture
from the grey stone walls, the lichen stains?

When she turned aside to face the setting sun
her auburn hair fell back
to show the lovebites on her neck.

I closed my eyes, appalled,
and when I opened them again
the diamond panes were clear.

III

Green lichen marks the flagstone
covering my grave.
No bells can ring
where I seep through the fen.

There are two who keep me company:
a red-haired girl to irk the shadow
at my door; and a bearded man who brings
news of politics and kings.

The girl stands in her shadow, hoping I may come,
being now no more
than waiting's phantom,
her cold in the northward facing stone.

The bearded man is kind.
His reddish hair enhances fresh and mottled skin;
a starched and snow-white ruff
upholds his courtier's head.

He turns to me to talk
but his voice is slowed down
to stress each word as if
it were a thread unpicked

from a tapestry of the possible,
the picker knowing he has the skill
to weave another set of chance
from the gathering riot of thread:

See that what you do
conforms to what occurs,
even as the tree bole stirs
to take upon itself a self that's new.

IV

The pale yellow of the primrose
thaws the dark green of the Spring.

Colours then go deepening, deepening,
until the small space of my grave
cannot hold me any more.

Come and search my tomb.

You will find that I have gone.

V

I am going the hundred yards
or so to Kilmalkedar church, its arch
a tension of the slotted years
in the lives of my parishioners.

The last one died
when I was twenty two,
a new recruit from Trinity College,
polished buckles on my shoes.

From behind the hedgerows
Catholic girls would peep. I could never tell
their faces from the flowers
they were always laughing through.

Now their tiny faces
crowd inside the pendant crowns
of the crimson fuchsia flowers.
In the autumn they are blood upon the road.

VI

Eventually I shall have been
a chink of daylight in a drystone wall;
a crevice in a rock;
mere weathering on
the grey stone of Kilmalkedar's arch.

And shall have been again
what I once became.

IT ALL MATTERS
(for Patrick Welch)

Everything is gathered on the green
on the Hangdog Road.
The Black Ash is a name for
saying over and over.

There is a small stone bridge
across a stream; pathways lead down
from the road to the water.
Man and boy wash a car.

A Ford Prefect. Every so often
the man goes down the pathway
to fill an enamel bucket. The load
swings on the holed wooden peg.

In sun the bodywork dries off
completely after drops
have been gathered by the leather.
Then the gleaming black is waxed.

A THEATRE FOR COLD BLUE
(for Roel Kaptein)

His anatomy was his theatre, a space
for watching himself; his mind
a tier of blue benches, rising, almost,
to the ceiling, set inside a perfect octahedron –
the walls of the dissecting room.

The roof was glass, fretted with filigree
metalwork to let in cool
eighteenth century light. He himself
was on the table, still
breathing, tense, ready for the inquiry.
He was his own surgeon for the students
and the onlookers, filleting secrecy.
When (this they were waiting for) he went into the brain
he opened stories moving through a field of colour:

    Grey light and wind, a flash
    of red petticoat above a seashore,
    a girl closing a heavy door
    on the afternoon aromatic
    with iodine and seaweed.

    Autumn, and he's reading going down
    the road; the air's
    all savour from the wrack.
    He looks up from words to see
    the haymakers in the field.
    An old man dressing the curve
    of the scythe in long strokes
    looks at him across the blade's arc,
    eyes clear as cold steel.

YOU KNEW IT

The house that waits
for me, for you,
has a small box hedge
running around the unkempt,
uncared for garden.

Bigger than you thought,
it has rooms you hoped
would not be there before you.
But there they are, in all their
trouble and damp grandeur.

You, and no one else,
you will have to try
to put this place to rights.
Outside, on the road, in sun,
a car flashes by, oblivious.

ON HE GOES

When he got there she had gone.
The yard was empty, the barn door
swung at an angle, one of the hinges
having cracked.

Where had he been all year?
Yesterday morning he woke,
his face in the grass, his breath white
above the blades stiff with frost.

He remembered a hovel,
four old women dressed in grey,
and a girl looking at him,
in silence.

He turned back down the road,
behind him the window panes
already starting to film
over with light green scum.

The sun was up. Beside him,
in the laneway the hawthorn
exhaled its milky smell; birds
singing in the branches made him sing out too.

UPPER EVERGREEN ROAD

Two streets met, at an angle of thirty degrees:
across the road a public house, tied
to Beamish's brewery; to the left
a limestone wall, settled, cool
and untroubled. On the corner
opposite the pub there was the potato store.
Spuds in jute sacks, with the nap
turned down, smelt of Nohoval,
Ballycotton, Youghal. Even here,
in the city, the faint tang of seaweed
which manured the crop. Right,
a little way up the street, a tiny shop
where the cobbler sat. When you came in
he looked up, his lips crammed with iron.

A VISIT TO FRANCIS STUART

Slowly he raised himself from the chair
and asked if I wanted some whiskey.
Soda, too, perhaps? The afternoon was calm.
I'd remarked, on the way in, the trench
dug for the seed potatoes; along the ridge of loose
earth was scattered a detritus
of last year's leaves and grass cuttings gathered
from the edges and the dry dark
underneath the privet. He asked me
to help myself when he put down the little tray.
Everything was careful and deliberate and neutral.
Imagine a conversation totally without opinion,
one from which all explanation is erased:
that was the nature of the conversation
we had at the back of our minds
when she came in, fabulous in Turkish trousers
of green silver. Pouring myself the second
(smaller) whiskey I looked through to the room beyond:
a lean-to, made of wood; a kitchen chair;
the part of the table I could see was strewn
with magazines and paper, writing materials.

Such a room, so easy of access,
just off, is a place for composing,
in the utmost lucidity and calm,
an alphabet of lovers, preliminary to
the vast compendium to be made of the soul's
resting places while she finds her way in time:
such as this very instant of possibility with
the trench dug, the seed potatoes soon to be set.

The place where you're going to have a go
at being yourself is the bleakest place you'll ever know.

ROBERT WELCH

Robert Welch was born in Cork city in 1947. He has been Professor of English at the University of Ulster, Coleraine, since 1984. He has lived and worked in Nigeria, Leeds, West Cork, and now lives on the north west coast, at Portstewart, with his wife and four children. His books include a study of nineteenth century Irish poetry, *Irish Poetry from Moore to Yeats,* a *History of Verse Translation from the Irish,* and a book on modern Irish writing, in English and Irish, to be called *Changing States,* due late 1991. He has edited various collections of essays, including one on George Moore, and another on *Irish Writers and Religion*; and has edited a volume in the Penguin Classics series of Yeats's writings, *W.B.Yeats: Writings on Irish Folklore, Legend and Myth,* due 1992. He is the editor of the *Oxford Companion to Irish Literature,* due 1993. He has lectured in France, Germany, Italy, Holland, Sweden, Austria, Japan, Hungary, Canada, the U.S., and Africa. *Muskerry* is his first collection of poems.